THINK BIG!

THE GREATEST IDEAS IN
MEDICINE

SONYA NEWLAND

WAYLAND

First published in Great Britain in 2022 by Wayland
Copyright © Wayland, 2022

Produced for Wayland by
White-Thomson Publishing Ltd
www.wtpub.co.uk

Editor: Sonya Newland
Designer: Rocket Design (East Anglia) Ltd

The publisher would like to thank the following for permission to reproduce their pictures:
Alamy: 4l (Science History Images), 12b (B Christopher), 20t (Martin Shields), 26b (Reuters), 27b (WENN Rights Ltd); Getty: 8b (Alfred Eisenstaedt), 10l, 10r, 16br (Bettmann), 13b (China News Service), 14r (Central Press), 20b (Universal Images Group Editorial), 22l, 29t (iStock), 23b (The Asahi Shimbun), 29b (Amber De Vos); Shutterstock:4r (itechno), 5b (Disobey Art), 5r (Zimny), 6l, 6r, 18t (Everett Collection), 7t (Nasky), 7b (Africa Studio), 8t (Kateryna Kon), 9t, 21t, 28b (Designua), 9b (i viewfinder), 11t (Dmitry Kalinovsky), 11b (Pszczola), 12t (April stock), 13t (Yoko Design), 14l (Okrasiuk), 15l (Macrovector), 15r (Olena Gaidarzhy), 16t (itsmejust), 16bl (samunella), 17t (Golden Sikorka), 17b (Tyler Olson), 18b (Michael D Brown), 19t (Talukdar David), 19b (MedstockPhotos), 21b (David A Litman), 22r (BlueRingMedia), 23t (Elena Pavlovich), 24l (RUCHUDA BOONPLIEN), 24r (UfaBizPhoto), 25t (mezzotint), 25b (yoojiwhan), 26t (Roman Zaiets), 27t (Crystal Eye Studio), 28t (Meletios Verras).

All design elements from Shutterstock.

Every attempt has been made to clear copyright. Should there be any inadvertent omission please apply to the publisher for rectification.

Printed in China

Wayland
An imprint of
Hachette Children's Group
Part of Hodder and Stoughton
Carmelite House
50 Victoria Embankment
London EC4Y 0DZ

An Hachette UK Company
www.hachette.co.uk
www.hachettechildrens.co.uk

Contents

Medicine

Since human history began, we have been using our ingenuity to prevent, treat and cure diseases, to fix things that go wrong with our bodies and to try to live longer, healthier lives.

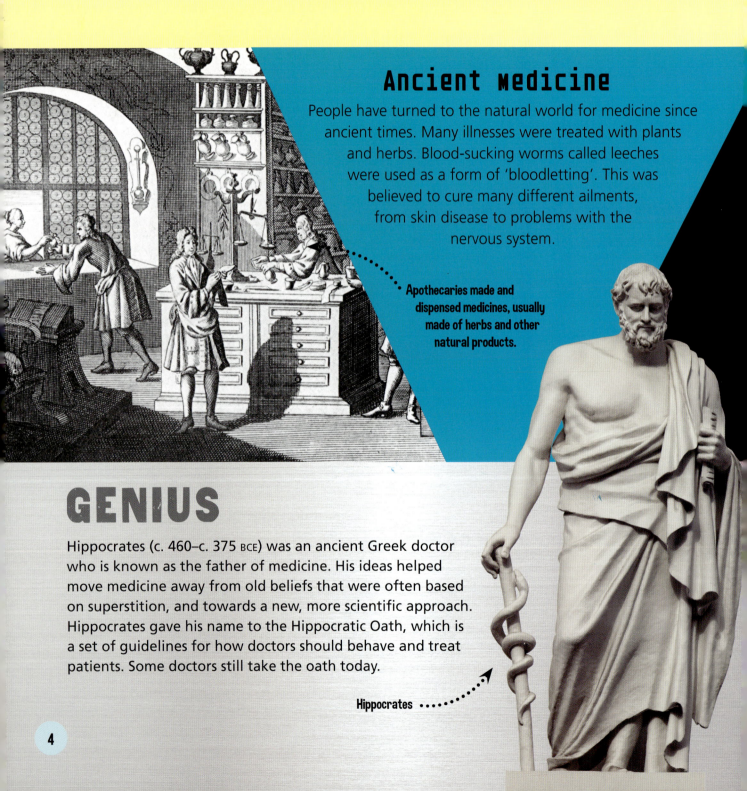

Ancient medicine

People have turned to the natural world for medicine since ancient times. Many illnesses were treated with plants and herbs. Blood-sucking worms called leeches were used as a form of 'bloodletting'. This was believed to cure many different ailments, from skin disease to problems with the nervous system.

Apothecaries made and dispensed medicines, usually made of herbs and other natural products.

GENIUS

Hippocrates (c. 460–c. 375 BCE) was an ancient Greek doctor who is known as the father of medicine. His ideas helped move medicine away from old beliefs that were often based on superstition, and towards a new, more scientific approach. Hippocrates gave his name to the Hippocratic Oath, which is a set of guidelines for how doctors should behave and treat patients. Some doctors still take the oath today.

Hippocrates

Operations

From ancient times, doctors attempted surgical procedures to fix more serious problems like broken bones. At first they used natural drugs, such as opium, to limit the pain of these operations. When anaesthetics were developed in the 1840s, surgery became much safer. Anaesthetics also allowed surgeons to perform much more complicated operations.

New technology

Both old and new ideas have led to the creation of technology and the introduction of techniques that have revolutionised medicine. This was particularly true in the 20th century – and into the 21st – when amazing developments in technology helped to advance medical science dramatically. This book explores some of the biggest ideas in medicine in recent times. Who knows how much more doctors will be able to do even a few years from now?

THINK BIG!

When COVID-19 first appeared in late 2019, it was known as a 'novel' coronavirus. That means it was a form of the virus that no one had seen before. It usually takes many years to create a vaccine for a new disease, but within a year of the COVID-19 outbreak, the first vaccines were being given to people. Find out which companies created successful vaccines. How did they do it? What testing and approval processes did the vaccines go through?

Social distancing and wearing masks were introduced in many places to limit the spread of COVID-19.

💊 The smallpox vaccine

Until the early 19th century, viruses could be easily caught and spread. Even if you didn't die from diseases caused by viruses, they could have terrible long-term effects. All that changed in 1796 thanks to English doctor Edward Jenner, who created the first vaccine.

The big idea

In the late 1700s, smallpox was a dangerous disease. Jenner noticed that milkmaids who caught the mild disease cowpox never caught smallpox. He wondered if catching cowpox made the human body immune to smallpox. To test his theory, he infected eight-year-old James Phipps with cowpox. A few weeks later, he injected Phipps with smallpox – but the boy did not develop the disease.

Jenner injected pus from a cowpox sore into a cut on a boy's arm to give him cowpox.

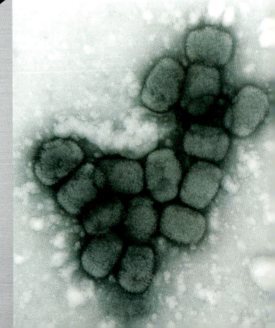

Smallpox is caused by the variola virus. This image shows the virus in the blood through a microscope.

GENIUS

Edward Jenner (1749–1823) was working as a doctor in a small English town when he made his discovery. He published his findings, but vaccination was not an immediate success. The cowpox samples used for the vaccine often got contaminated, and some other doctors did not want Jenner to succeed. Eventually, however, people realised how many lives could be saved by vaccination, and Jenner became highly respected.

The vaccine is usually given in liquid form, as an injection.

Instead of giving the person the disease, the opposite happens: the antigens make the body create antibodies in the blood.

Antibodies are part of the immune system, and they fight off the disease if the person gets it in the future.

How does it work?

Vaccines work by giving people a tiny dose of antigens, which are part of the virus that cause an illness. These are usually very weak, or even dead, versions of the disease.

Where did it lead?

Today, there are vaccines to stop us catching and spreading a whole host of diseases. There are vaccines for dangerous childhood diseases such as measles and mumps, as well as a vaccine for the flu, a virus that can be dangerous for many people. Vaccines have been so successful that some diseases, including smallpox, have been completely eradicated.

THINK BIG!

Dangerous diseases such as cholera, diphtheria, tetanus, hepatitis A and whooping cough still exist, even though there are vaccines for them. Research one of these diseases and find out what causes it. Where in the world it is a problem and why? When was the vaccine developed and what vaccine programmes are now in place? Why do you think it is important that this disease should be eradicated?

Antibiotics

Before antibiotics, infections caused by bacteria could be extremely dangerous. Bacteria multiply and spread quickly, so even a small scratch can cause a nasty infection. Today, bacterial infections can be treated easily — but amazingly, the age of antibiotics began with an accidental discovery.

The big idea

In 1928, Scottish scientist Alexander Fleming (1881–1955) returned to his laboratory after a holiday to find that mould had built up in the dishes containing the bacteria he was studying. He noticed a curious thing: the bacteria, staphylococcus, had not spread into the parts of the dish where the mould was. Fleming discovered that a substance called penicillin was stopping the bacteria growing. He realised that if pure penicillin could be isolated, it could be used as a medicine to treat bacterial infections.

Fleming discovered that his 'mould juice' could kill many types of bacteria.

GENIUS

Fleming found that extracting penicillin was a slow and expensive process. Not enough could be produced to make it a useful medicine. It was not until 1941 that Howard Florey (1898–1968) and Ernst Chain (1906–79) found a way of mass-producing penicillin. Their extraction process meant that the life-saving antibiotic drug was soon widely available.

In 1945, Fleming (pictured), Florey and Chain were jointly awarded the Nobel Prize in Physiology or Medicine for their work on penicillin.

How does it work?

Today, there are many types of antibiotic. They cure infections either by killing the bacteria or by slowing and eventually stopping them from multiplying. Antibiotics can do this in different ways.

Antibiotics block the bacteria from producing proteins.

They stop DNA in the bacteria cell from replicating.

They attack the cell wall so it is not strong enough to survive in the human body.

They affect the cell membrane, which controls how substances get in and out of the cell.

They block the bacteria from producing a vitamin it needs, folic acid.

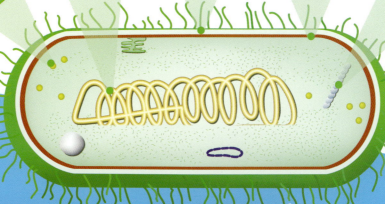

Antibiotics are now available as pills, ointments or liquids.

Where did it lead?

Penicillin arrived just in time to save the lives of countless soldiers during the Second World War (1939–45). Before the war, 30 per cent of all deaths were due to bacterial infections. This dropped dramatically, as people were prescribed penicillin. Today, antibiotics are a common treatment for both mild and serious infections.

THINK BIG!

One of the problems with antibiotics is that bacteria can develop resistance to them. That means the bacteria 'fight back' against the antibiotics. Do some research to find out how bacteria develop resistance and why this is a problem. What big ideas are scientists researching to overcome this problem?

Transplant surgery

Your vital organs are the parts of your body that are essential for survival. They include your heart, kidney, liver and lungs. Until the mid-20th century, if one of these organs stopped working properly, the person usually died. So, when doctors found a way of replacing a damaged organ with one from another person, it was literally a life-saver.

The big idea

For years, doctors and scientists worked on ways to replace organs in the body that had been damaged beyond repair, but transplant surgery was extremely complicated. There was also a high chance that the patient's body would reject the new organ. Despite these obstacles, the first successful transplant surgery took place in 1954, when a kidney from one twin was transplanted into his brother.

GENIUS

Christiaan Barnard (1922–2001) was the South African heart surgeon who performed the first successful heart transplant, in 1967. The patient died a few weeks later, from complications with the drugs he was given to stop his body rejecting the new heart. Improvements were soon made to these drugs, and Barnard went on to become a leading transplant surgeon.

Christiaan Barnard

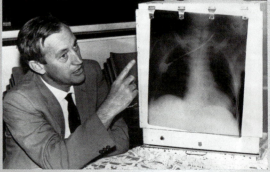

Throughout the 1960s, other successful organ transplants were achieved with the heart, lungs and pancreas.

How does it work?

A lot of things have to be just right for an organ transplant to work. The donor organ usually has to come from someone with the same blood type as the patient (or from someone who has blood type O). Some organs, such as hearts, can come only from people who have died, but many other transplants are now done using live donors.

In 2018, nearly 150,000 organ transplants took place worldwide.

Where did it lead?

Today, many different parts of the body can be successfully transplanted, from hearts to body tissue to corneas in the eye. Transplanting major organs is still serious surgery and carries risks, but success rates are improving every year as scientists learn more, and as technology for surgery improves. People can choose to be organ donors, so when they die their organs are used to help other people. Just one donor can save the lives of up to eight people.

Some of the most common transplants are:

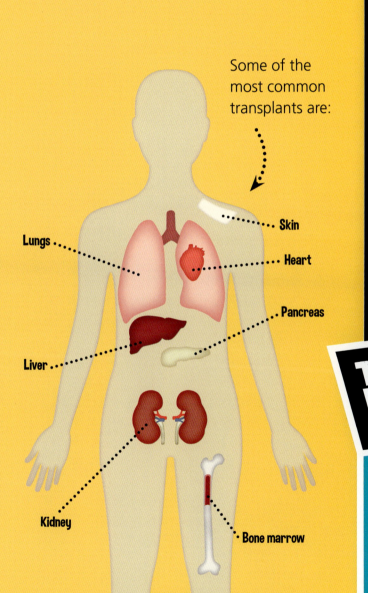

Lungs

Skin

Heart

Pancreas

Liver

Kidney

Bone marrow

THINK BIG!

Do some research to find out why blood is an important part of transplant surgery. How can being a blood donor help people who need transplants and other types of surgery? What is involved in donating blood? Think of ways you could raise awareness of the importance of adults becoming blood donors.

Pacemakers

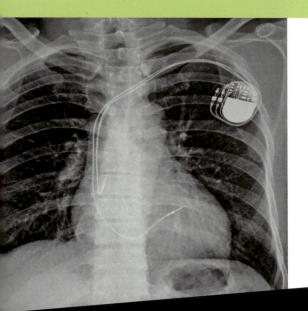

Each time your heart beats, its muscle contracts, ready to pump blood around the body. Normally, the heart beats in a regular rhythm, but some medical conditions can cause an abnormal heartbeat. A device called a pacemaker implanted in the body can detect when the heartbeat is abnormal and get the heart beating regularly again.

The big idea

One day, electrical engineer Wilson Greatbatch accidentally put part of an electrical circuit in the wrong way round, causing an electrical pulse. This reminded Greatbatch of a medical problem he had heard about called 'heart block', where the heart beats more slowly or irregularly than usual. Greatbatch realised that the electrical pulse he had created could imitate a heartbeat.

GENIUS

Wilson Greatbatch (1919–2011) was an American engineer and inventor. Over his lifetime, he was granted patents for more than 300 big ideas, including a special lithium-iodide battery that could be used in pacemakers. Greatbatch won many honours for his work in a wide range of areas, from medical research to renewable energy.

The Chardack-Greatbatch pacemaker was named after Greatbatch and heart surgeon William Chardack (1914–2006), who helped him design the first implantable device.

How does it work?

The contractions in the heart are caused by natural electrical impulses. A pacemaker uses artificial impulses to keep the heart beating in a regular rhythm.

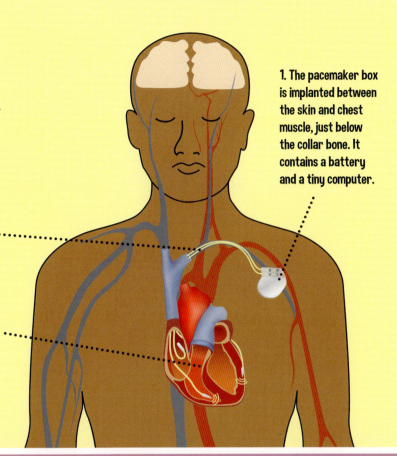

1. The pacemaker box is implanted between the skin and chest muscle, just below the collar bone. It contains a battery and a tiny computer.

2. One or two wires attached to the box are fed through the veins into the right side of the heart.

3. The wires sense what the heart is doing. If the heart slows down or misses a beat, the box sends out electrical impulses to set the heart's rhythm right again.

Where did it lead?

Although early pacemakers could be implanted successfully, they didn't last very long. Most needed replacing every two or three years. Today, however, battery life is much better and pacemakers last for many years. More than three million people now rely on them to keep their hearts beating regularly, and hundreds of thousands more are implanted every year.

Technology is now so advanced that a new wireless type of pacemaker is being developed that can be implanted directly into the heart.

THINK BIG!

How else could technology be used in medicine? Think like Wilson Greatbatch and try to come up with a device that could help control a part of the human body. Draw a diagram to show how your invention would work. Consider what problems there might be when using it, then try to work out how they could be solved.

In vitro fertilisation (IVF)

While many people conceive children naturally, others have difficulty getting pregnant. In vitro fertilisation (IVF) is a process in which an egg is fertilised to create a human embryo outside the body. It is then put inside the woman, where it can develop into a baby as normal.

The big idea

By the 1960s, experts had managed to fertilise animal eggs outside the body, but no one was sure it would work for humans. Scientist Robert Edwards, doctor Patrick Steptoe and nurse Jean Purdy believed it could be done. They came up with an experimental treatment and asked for volunteers to be part of a trial. Hundreds of women applied!

Many people disagreed with the idea of IVF at first, because they felt it was 'unnatural', and that human life should not be created in a laboratory.

GENIUS

British team Edwards (1925–2013), Steptoe (1913–88) and Purdy (1945–85) were the pioneers of IVF. Steptoe had established a way of gathering eggs using an instrument called a laparoscope. Edwards developed a way of fertilising the eggs in a laboratory. Purdy was the world's first clinical embryologist. After their first successful programme, they began training other doctors in the process to help thousands of childless couples.

Jean Purdy, seen here with Edwards, helped to develop the IVF process.

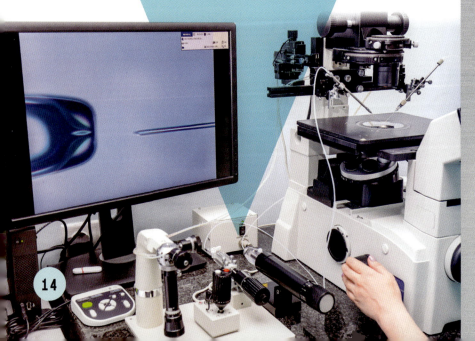

How does it work?

The basic process for IVF treatment is the same today as it was when Edwards, Steptoe and Purdy set up their programme.

Where did it lead?

In 1978, Louise Brown became the first baby to be born from IVF. By this time, the team had set up a private clinic to deal with the demand for their treatment, and soon many more people were expecting IVF babies. Millions of babies have now been born from IVF treatment.

A woman is given hormones that make her ovaries produce several eggs.

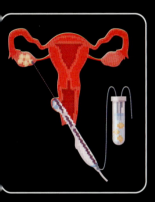

The eggs are collected from the woman's ovaries.

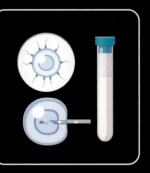

They are fertilised in a laboratory, using the man's sperm. They may be mixed together to fertilise naturally, or a single sperm may be injected into an egg.

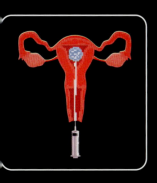

If one or more eggs are successfully fertilised, the embryos are left to develop for two to six days before one is implanted back into the woman's uterus.

THINK BIG!

Multiple births, such as twins and triplets, occur much more frequently as a result of IVF treatment than they do naturally. Find out why. Do you think doctors should research ways to ensure that only one baby at a time is born from IVF? Why, or why not?

MRI scanning

Before the late 19th century, doctors had to rely on symptoms to diagnose disease, and the only way to see inside the body was to cut it open. The discovery of X-rays in 1895 set diagnostic medicine on a new path. But it was the development of scanning techniques in the 1970s that marked a great leap forward in this area.

 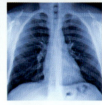 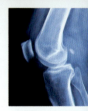
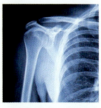 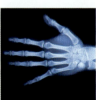 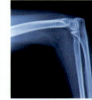
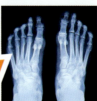

X-rays are usually used to identify problems with the bones and joints, such as breaks.

The big idea

Earlier technologies like X-rays and CT scanning allowed doctors to look inside a patient's body without invasive surgery. Magnetic resonance imaging (MRI) was a scanning technique that developed these ideas. Unlike X-rays, MRI could create images of soft tissues, such as the organs and blood vessels. This meant it could diagnose a whole range of different diseases.

GENIUS

American doctor Raymond Damadian (b. 1936) was the first to realise that MRI imaging could change the way doctors diagnosed diseases, especially forms of cancer. He invented the MRI scanner in 1972, and later worked with Wilson Greatbatch (see page 12) to create a pacemaker that could be safely used in an MRI scanner.

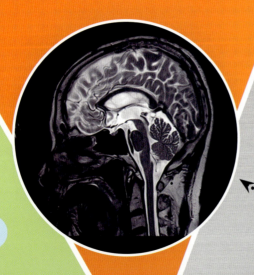

An MRI image of the brain.

Raymond Damadian

How does it work?

An MRI scanner uses magnetic fields and radio waves to create images of the inside of the body and even the brain.

An MRI scanner is a large metal tube.

The magnetic field and radio waves change the 'spin' of particles called protons in the body.

The scanner measures this signal and converts it into an image on a linked computer.

When the magnetic field is turned off, the particles return to their normal spin. As they do so, they create a radio signal.

The patient lies on a bed inside the scanner.

Where did it lead?

The first MRI scanners were noisy, and the process took a long time. In the past 30 years, MRI technology has improved a lot. A scan takes 20–90 minutes, depending on the size of the area being scanned. The image quality is also much better, so doctors can diagnose problems more accurately.

More than 3.5 million MRI scans are carried out each year in the UK alone.

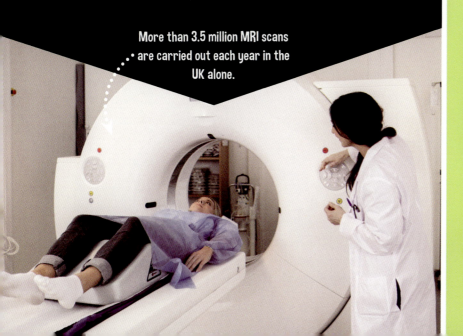

THINK BIG!

Look online to find out what the difference is between CT scanners and MRI scanners. What kind of images do they create? What are the advantages of each type of scan? What are they used for? Can you think of any ways either of them could be improved? What type of imaging might there be in the future?

The Global Polio Eradication Initiative

Poliomyelitis – better known as polio – is an infectious disease that often affects children. If the virus gets into the spinal cord it can paralyse the patient. The Global Polio Eradication Initiative (GPEI) was established to tackle this terrible disease.

An 'iron lung' was a life-support machine that helped polio victims breathe if their lungs had been paralysed.

The big idea

In developed nations, polio was brought under control in the 1960s. But in other parts of the world it still causes death or permanent disability in thousands of children. In 1988, six organisations, including the World Health Organization (WHO) and the Bill & Melinda Gates Foundation, came together as the Global Polio Eradication Initiative, with one aim: to make polio a disease of the past everywhere in the world.

How does it work?

A vaccine exists for polio, so the GPEI's strategy was to create herd immunity. If most of the population is immunised, the disease is contained because there are enough immune people to stop it being transmitted to those who aren't immune. The programme focused on the worst-affected countries: Afghanistan, Pakistan and Nigeria.

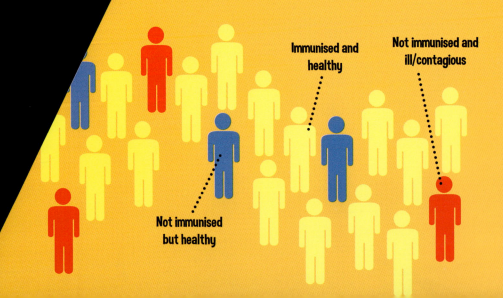

Immunised and healthy

Not immunised and ill/contagious

Not immunised but healthy

Where did it lead?

Cases of polio worldwide have dropped dramatically. In fact, certain forms of the virus have now been completely eradicated. Diseases can be unpredictable, and in 2019 there was a surge of polio cases in Afghanistan and Pakistan. But the GPEI is still working towards what it calls the 'endgame' – a polio-free world.

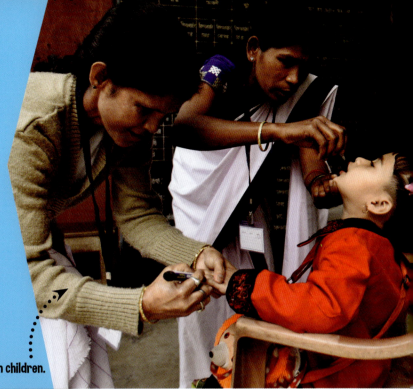

So far, the programme has vaccinated more than 2.5 billion children.

GENIUS

As the son of a Jamaican man and a white English woman, pathologist Alan Goffe (1920–66) faced racial discrimination in the world of medicine in the 1950s and 1960s. Despite this, he played an important part in developing and improving the vaccines for polio and measles. His work to make the vaccines safe for millions of people was so important that a type of measles was named the 'Goffe strain' after him.

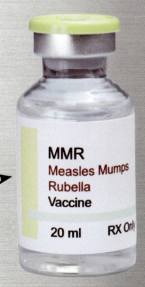

The MMR vaccine protects against three childhood diseases: measles, mumps and rubella.

If you could form an organisation of governments, scientists and medical experts with the aim of eradicating one disease from the world, what would it be and why? Find out if there are any groups – large or small – that are already working on this problem, and see if there is anything you could do to contribute, such as raising awareness of the disease.

The Human Genome Project

Our genetic material is the stuff inside us that makes us grow and develop. During the second half of the 20th century, scientists began to find out more about genes and DNA. They started to wonder if it was possible to map and understand all the genes in the human body (the 'genome').

The big idea

The Human Genome Project (HGP) was an international research programme established in 1990. DNA is made up of units called bases. The aim of the HGP was to work out the sequence of every DNA base in the human genome, and to identify every gene in our bodies. When it started, the HGP was given 15 years and a budget of US$3 billion – and amazingly, it achieved its goal early and under budget!

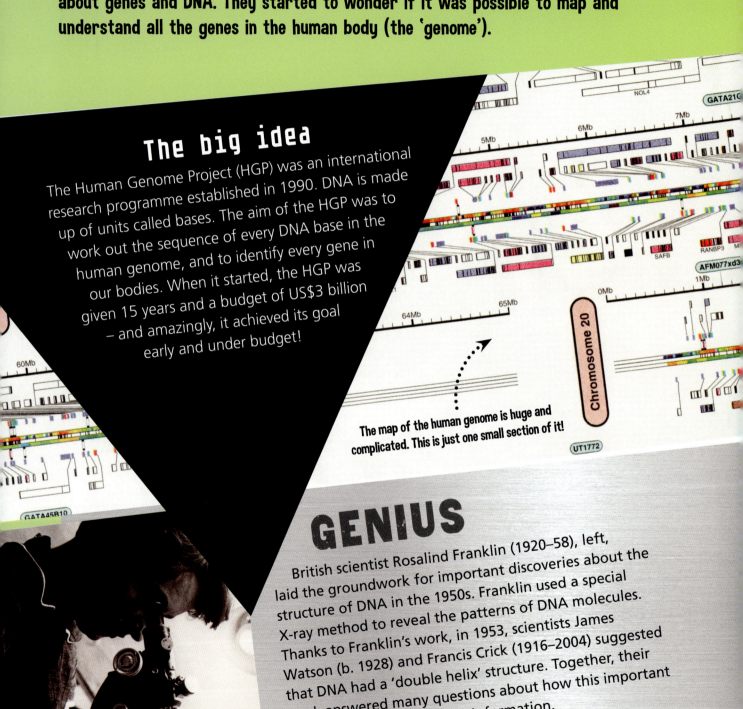

The map of the human genome is huge and complicated. This is just one small section of it!

GENIUS

British scientist Rosalind Franklin (1920–58), left, laid the groundwork for important discoveries about the structure of DNA in the 1950s. Franklin used a special X-ray method to reveal the patterns of DNA molecules. Thanks to Franklin's work, in 1953, scientists James Watson (b. 1928) and Francis Crick (1916–2004) suggested that DNA had a 'double helix' structure. Together, their work answered many questions about how this important molecule carries hereditary information.

Chromosomes, DNA and genes

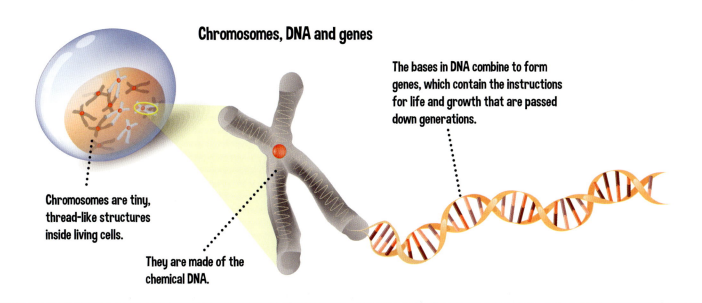

Chromosomes are tiny, thread-like structures inside living cells.

They are made of the chemical DNA.

The bases in DNA combine to form genes, which contain the instructions for life and growth that are passed down generations.

How did it work?

Scientists at the HGP divided DNA into small sections so computers could work out the order of the bases in each section. From there, they could figure out which bases made up genes and which didn't. There are about 30,000 genes in the human genome.

Where did it lead?

An accurate human genome sequence was completed in 2003. It was a massive achievement that benefited science and medicine in many ways. For example, understanding the human genome will help researchers know more about – and treat – hereditary diseases, such as sickle cell disease and haemophilia, and genetic disorders such as cystic fibrosis.

Find out more about how genes function in the human body. Being able to identify and manipulate genes can have great medical advantages, but what might be the disadvantages? Could we start changing characteristics that are really only desirable, not essential for health? Where would you draw the line?

Scientists have sequenced the DNA in cancer cells like these. By comparing this sequence with the sequence completed by the HGP, they can work out which genes are causing the disease.

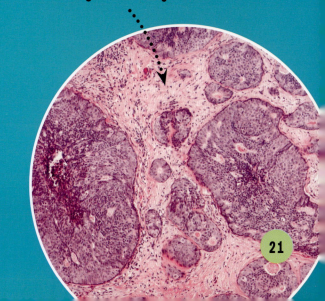

21

Stem cells are unique in the human body, because they can divide and specialise. For example, stem cells can become blood cells, skin cells, nerve cells or the cells of different organs like the liver. If scientists can manipulate stem cells to become particular types of cell, the cells can be used to repair damage to our bodies.

The big idea

There are two types of natural stem cell. In an embryo, most cells are stem cells, because they haven't yet differentiated, or changed, into specialised cells. Some stem cells remain undifferentiated. These 'adult stem cells' maintain and repair specialised cells when necessary. Most research uses embryonic stem cells, because they can be manipulated more easily.

Stem cells can keep making new stem cells through cell division.

How does it work?

In stem cell therapy, researchers grow stem cells in a laboratory. They manipulate them so they specialise into a particular type of cell, such as liver cells or heart muscle cells. These cells are then transplanted (usually by injection) into someone who has a damaged liver or heart muscle. The new, healthy cells help repair the damaged body part.

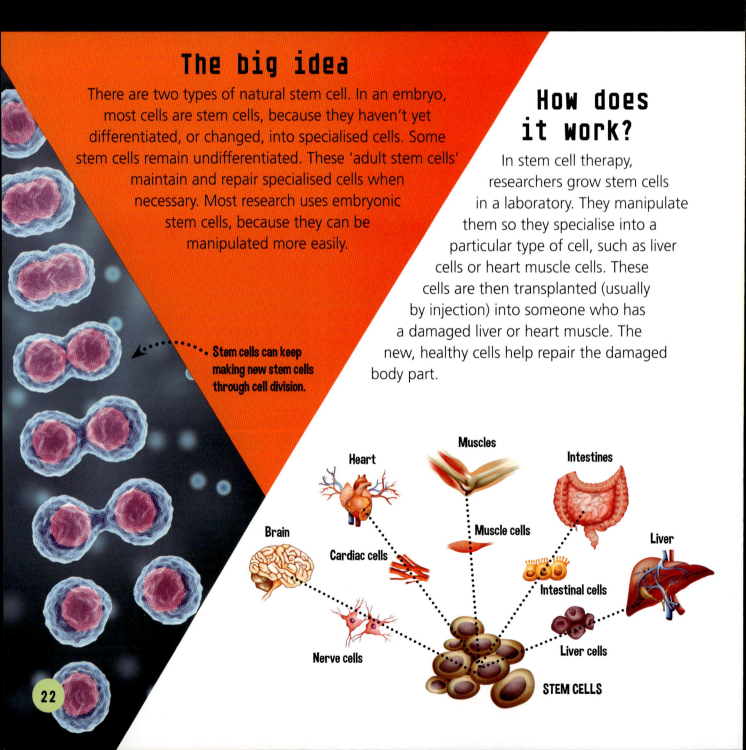

Brain
Heart
Muscles
Intestines
Liver
Cardiac cells
Muscle cells
Intestinal cells
Nerve cells
Liver cells
STEM CELLS

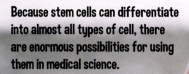

Because stem cells can differentiate into almost all types of cell, there are enormous possibilities for using them in medical science.

Where will it lead?

Stem cells have the potential to treat many medical issues, including heart disease, spinal damage and diabetes, as well as brain disorders such as Alzheimer's disease. Some cancers, such as leukaemia, may already respond to a bone marrow transplant, which is a stem cell treatment. Researchers are working on ways to generate blood cells from stem cells. They hope to one day find a way to create a limitless supply of blood that can be used in transfusions.

THINK BIG!

Choose from liver cells, heart cells, red blood cells, white blood cells, nerve cells or skin cells. Find out what benefits there would be to turning stem cells into your chosen cell type and transplanting them. What disease could be cured? What conditions could be eradicated? What damage could be repaired? Find out if any research is already being done in this area.

GENIUS

Japanese biologist Shinya Yamanaka (b. 1962) shared the 2012 Nobel Prize for Medicine for his research on adult stem cells. Yamanaka and his team had found a way of turning a type of specialised adult cell back into a stem cell. These changed cells, called induced pluripotent stem cells (iPS cells), behave like embryonic stem cells. This breakthrough could revolutionise stem cell treatments.

Bionic prosthetics

Humans have been creating artificial body parts for thousands of years — wooden toes have even been discovered in ancient Egypt! But today's artificial limbs are incredible pieces of medical engineering. Bionic prosthetics are artificial body parts that move using signals from the brain, muscles and nerves.

The big idea

Ordinary prosthetic limbs allow people with physical disabilities to move more freely than they would on crutches or in wheelchairs. However, these limbs can still be cumbersome. Experts wanted to create prosthetics that had the range of movement and worked in the same instinctive way as real limbs. To do so, they needed to harness the body's own electrical system.

A user puts on a bionic lower arm and flexes the muscles in their real upper arm.

Traditional artificial limbs are designed to look like the real thing, but they have limited movement and control.

How do they work?

All our movements are controlled by electrical signals from the brain. Bionic prosthetics use a technology called electromyography. This picks up signals from the user's muscles in a similar way to a real limb. Users have to learn to control the signals, but most find they get used to this very quickly.

Where did it lead?

The first bionic limb was fitted in 1998, but technology has since developed rapidly. Today, bionic prosthetic limbs use cutting-edge science and technology. Many are made from carbon fibre, which is light, strong and long-lasting. Sensors respond to instructions from the brain in fractions of a second. Researchers are also finding ways to restore feeling into missing limbs, sending sensations from the artificial part back to the brain.

Many athletes in high-level competitions such as the Paralympics have bionic limbs.

GENIUS

As a teenager in the United States, Easton LaChappelle (b. 1996) met a girl who had a prosthetic arm. The limb had cost her family a huge amount of money and would need to be replaced several times as she grew up. This inspired Easton to create a revolutionary 3D printed bionic arm that could be controlled by the mind. He now runs his own company, Unlimited Tomorrow, which develops robotics that will have a positive impact on people's lives.

THINK BIG!

Design your own prosthetic body part. It doesn't have to be an arm or a leg – think about fingers, toes or even eyes. Consider all the different ways that your chosen part moves and what its functions are. How realistically could you recreate these movements and functions in an artificial part? What would be the most important features of your prosthetic? Perhaps you could even improve how the real body parts work!

Remote surgery

Using robots to perform surgery isn't a new idea, and robotics are quite common in operating theatres. But remote surgery, or telesurgery, takes this technology to a whole new level, allowing surgeons to perform procedures without being in the same room as the patient.

Surgeons already use robotic instruments, which are less invasive than in traditional surgeries.

The big idea

As robotics and communications technology improved in the late 20th century, scientists began exploring ways to perform surgery from a distance. The idea became a reality in 2001, when the first remote surgery was performed. A surgeon in New York, USA, performed an operation on a woman nearly 6,500 km away in France, using a robotic system called Zeus.

GENIUS

French doctor Jacques Marescaux (b. 1948) was the surgeon who performed the first remote surgery. He is a pioneer of using digital technology in medical procedures, and teaches young doctors how to do this at the University of Strasbourg. Marescaux is also president of IRCAD, an organisation that researches cancer of the digestive system.

Jacques Marescaux

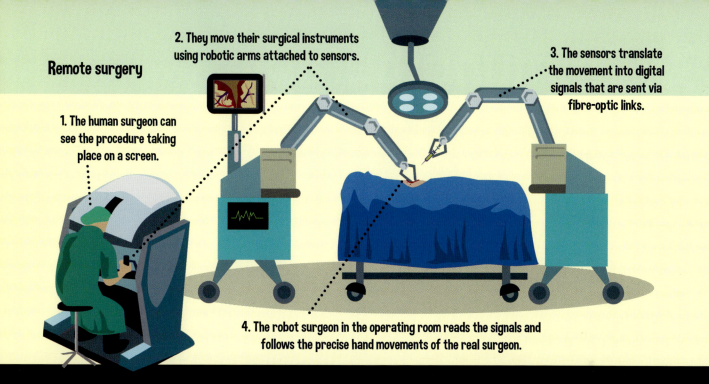

Remote surgery

1. The human surgeon can see the procedure taking place on a screen.

2. They move their surgical instruments using robotic arms attached to sensors.

3. The sensors translate the movement into digital signals that are sent via fibre-optic links.

4. The robot surgeon in the operating room reads the signals and follows the precise hand movements of the real surgeon.

How does it work?

A robotic surgical system is usually made up of two robotic arms, a main console and a system of sensors that sends feedback to the surgeon (see diagram above).

Where will it lead?

Remote surgery has huge benefits. There are not enough specialist surgeons in many areas of medicine, so being able to perform operations remotely means that more people can be treated. It also gives people access to treatments who would not otherwise have it, such as those who live in developing countries. As robotic technology develops, the type of surgery that can be performed remotely will become more advanced.

Robotics and artificial intelligence (AI) are fast-growing area of technology that have made remote surgery possible. How else might these technologies be used? Design a robot or an intelligent system that can help in another area of medicine or health. You could find out what research is already being carried out in these areas to give you some ideas.

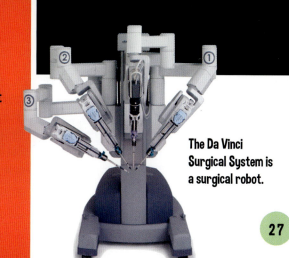

The Da Vinci Surgical System is a surgical robot.

✸ Immunotherapy

Your immune system is what protects you from infection and disease. It is made up of cells, tissues and organs that fight back when you get an infection. But cancer cells are clever — they can hide from and confuse the immune system. Immunotherapy uses the body's immune system to find and destroy the cancerous cells.

The big idea

Over many years, researchers have found different ways of treating cancer, including chemotherapy and radiation therapy. But many specialists are convinced that the best way of beating cancer is to train the immune system to get better at finding and fighting the diseased cells. This type of treatment is known as immunotherapy.

How does it work?

There are different types of immunotherapy. Two examples are CAR T-cell transfer therapy and checkpoint inhibitors.

CAR T-cell transfer therapy

T-cells are a type of white blood cell that are key to the immune system. In CAR T-cell transfer therapy, the body's natural immune cells are taken from the site of the cancer. Lots of these T-cells are grown in a laboratory and given a special protein called CAR. They are then injected back into the patient, boosting the immune system.

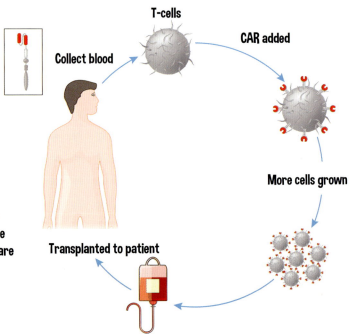

Collect blood

T-cells

CAR added

More cells grown

Transplanted to patient

Checkpoint inhibitors

T-cell

Antigen

Inhibitors

Cancer cell

Checkpoint inhibitors are drugs that block immune 'checkpoints'. These are a normal part of the immune system that stop it fighting too hard against an infection. Blocking the checkpoints allows the immune system to react much more strongly when it detects cancer cells.

Where will it lead?

In 2014, CAR T-cell therapy was recorded to have a 92 per cent response rate. Successes like this show that immunotherapies could be a game-changer in cancer treatments. Immunotherapy researchers are now working on developing drugs and other treatments for many types of cancer. One day, immunotherapy may even lead to a cure for cancer.

GENIUS

Indo-Guyanese scientist Padmanee Sharma (b. 1970) is a leading immunologist researcher. In 2003, she won an ASCO Young Investigator Award for identifying a 'marker' in some types of bladder cancer that could help the immune system's T-cells target the cancer cells. Since then, Sharma has continued to find ways of improving the effectiveness of immunotherapy treatments for cancers.

Padmanee Sharma

THINK BIG!

Why do you think stem cells (see pages 22–23) might be useful in immunotherapy? See if you can come up with your own big idea for how they might be used. You could start by looking online for information about young scientist Gabriel Dayan, who won an award for his ideas on using stem cells to boost the immune system.

Glossary

abnormal describes things that look or behave in a way that is different from normal

anaesthetic a substance that blocks our sensitivity to pain

antibody a substance produced by the immune system that can fight antigens to stop people getting a disease

antigen the part of a germ that can cause disease

bacteria tiny, single-celled organisms

DNA the molecule in living things that contains all the information about how they look and function

donor organ in a transplant, the healthy organ that is used to replace the damaged one

embryo the first stage of development of an unborn baby

eradicated to be completely destroyed

fertilisation the joining of an egg and a sperm at the start of the process of reproduction

hereditary describing characteristics that we inherit from our parents

hormones substances in the body that tell body parts what to do, such as grow or stop growing

immune able to resist infection from disease

immune system the system in the human body that fights diseases

laparoscope a long, very thin medical instrument that can be inserted inside the body to perform minor operations

mass-producing making something on a large scale, usually in a factory

Nobel Prize an international award given to people who have made an important contribution to different areas, including physics, literature, medicine and peace

ovary the organ in a woman's body where eggs are produced

pancreas an organ that sits behind the stomach in the body, which produces substances called enzymes that help us digest food

patent a licence granting someone ownership of an invention, which stops other people making and selling the same idea

pathologist a scientist who studies the cause of diseases

pioneer a person who leads the way in something

replicating reproducing an exact copy of something

transfusion when donated blood is put into someone's body

vaccine a method of stopping people catching a disease by injecting them with a very mild form of the virus that causes it

virus a tiny germ that causes disease if it gets inside the body

Further information

Books

A Short, Illustrated History of Medicine by John C. Miles (Franklin Watts, 2021)

Cutting-edge Medicine (Discover) by Meg Marquardt (Lerner Publications, 2016)

What's Next for Medicine? (Future Science Now) by Tom Jackson (Wayland, 2015)

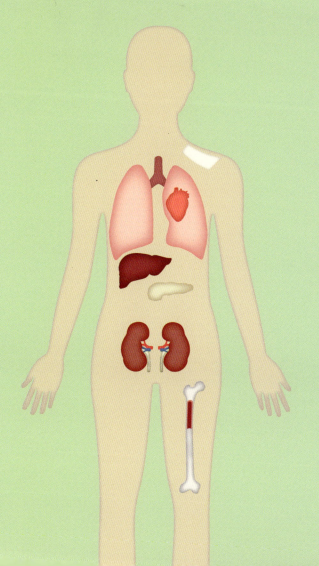

Websites

www.genome.gov/human-genome-project

Find out how the Human Genome Project worked and what it discovered.

polioeradication.org/

Explore the website of the Global Polio Eradication Initiative to find out about their latest campaigns and success stories.

www.yourgenome.org/facts/what-is-a-stem-cell

Discover more about stem cells: what they are, why they are so useful and where the research is taking us.

www.youtube.com/watch?v=CfmNXPMjChs

Watch whiz-kid Easton LaChappelle give a TED Talk about his prosthetic limb design.

The website addresses (URLs) included in this book were valid at the time of going to press. However, it is possible that contents or addresses may have changed since the publication of this book. No responsibility for any such changes can be accepted by either the author or the publisher.

Index